Asgar Zeynalov

Victor Hugo's Eastern View

RB

Rossendale Books

Published by Rossendale Books
57 Bedford Square,
LONDON
WC1B 3DP
England

Published in paperback 2016
Category: Literature
Copyright Asgar Zeynalov © 2016
ISBN : 978-1-365-22351-8

The great French writer Victor Hugo said at the funeral of his friend on 20 August 1850, "Balzac was one of that powerful generation of writers of the XIX century who came after Napoleon..." Victor Hugo was also one of that powerful generation of writers of the XIX-century French literature who came after Napoleon.

Asgar ZEYNALOV

In a speech to mark the centenary of Voltaire's death in 1878, Victor Hugo said: "He was not just a person. He was a century." The same words can be attributed to Victor Hugo as well.

Asgar ZEYNALOV

The translator of the book:
doctor of philology Fiala ABDULLAYEVA

Chief editor: *Sabina ZEYNALOVA*

Reviewers: *Doctor of philology Qorkhmaz QULIYEV*
Doctor of philology Vazeh ASGEROV

Artist: *Sakina ZEYNALOVA*

This book by PhD Asgar Zeynalov has been devoted to Victor Hugo's creative activity. The monograph deals with the French writer's life, the Azerbaijani translation of his works and their studies. It presents the analysis of Hugo's collection of poems "Les Orientales", his verses dedicated to the death of his daughter Leopoldine as well as the novels "The Hunchback of Notre Dame" and "Les Miserables". The book also touches upon the lives and creative activities of the writers, who were Hugo's contemporaries.

Table of contents

PREFACE

ASGAR ZEYNALOV
(Preface to the English translation of the monograph)

Asgar Mammad oghlu Zeynalov was born in the village of Yukhari Nejili of the Ulukhanli district not far from Irevan on 27 September 1951. He graduated from the French Faculty of Azerbaijan University of Languages in 1974. PhD and member of the Azerbaijan Union of Writers and Journalists, Asgar Zeynalov is the author of more than 30 books and over 350 scientific and journalistic articles. He has published articles in Iran, Turkey and Moscow, also books in St. Petersburg (2011), Moscow (2013), France (2015), Germany (2016) and USA (2016). The first monographs about Voltaire and Hugo in the Azerbaijani literary studies belong to A. Zeynalov. In 2003 he defended his doctoral thesis on "The East in French Literature" (on the basis of Voltaire's creative activity).

In 2014 his monograph "Hugo" was submitted to the State Prize of the Republic of Azerbaijan. A. Zeynalov is well known as the scholar specialized in French literature, especially in Hugo in France as well. The outstanding French scholar Jean Louis Bacque-Grammont wrote a review to his monograph "The East in French Literature" (1997). The newspaper "L'Est Republicain" published articles about A. Zeynalov as a Hugo specialist on 11 August 2007 and 24 July 2014. Arnaud Laster, the President of the Society of Hugo's Friends contributed an article about the Azerbaijani scholar to the bulletin of the Society in Paris in 2013. The literary scholar A. Zeynalov published articles on La Fountaine, Voltaire, Hugo, Balzac, Stendhal, Dumas, George Sand, Flaubert, Merimee and Maupassant at different times. At present he works at Azerbaijan University of Languages.

THE ORIENTAL MOTIVES IN VICTOR HUGO'S POETRY

W hile Europe has long been interested in the East, as it is pointed out by the researchers, only the late XVIII century saw the formation of a new science, Oriental Studies; societies began to appear in Europe in the late XVIII century.

The XVIII century carried out its decent task of introducing the East to Europe. Especially, through two important events: through the translations of "The Arabian Nights" and "Avesta". However, one cannot but mention the works written on the theme of the East in Europe in that period either. The researcher I.M.Kessel, who deals with the works created on the Oriental theme in those countries in different centuries, wrote, "These literary facts state that Western literature was being enriched with Oriental characters from century to century".

What was the situation like in the XIX-century European literature in this regard?

First, it should be mentioned that while in the XIX-century West the most significant works related to the Oriental themes were mainly created in France, the XIX century saw the appearance of strong pieces of art on this theme in different countries. Among them, one should especially mention two works, the British poet Byron's "Oriental Tales" (1813-1816), the German poet Goethe's "West-Eastern Diwan" (1819). However, besides this, H.T.Moore, V.Rott, T.Hop, H.Heine, J.Morier and other artists in European literature created their works on or related to the East. What was the situation like in French literature in this period?

In the XIX-century French literature the interest in the East, the appeal to the Oriental themes extended its scopes ever more. In that century, most French writers and poets created their works on the Oriental themes or related to the East: Chateaubriand, Jule Verne, Lamartine, Gotye, George Sand, and Balzac. It should be admitted that none of the works created in this period could attract the attention as much as "The Persian Letters", "Zadig" and "Zair".

The outstanding writer Victor Hugo was one of the representatives of the XIX-century French literature who turned to this theme. Hugo, who was one of the irreplaceable giants of world literature, wrote his poems on this topic in 1826-1828 and published them as a book titled "Les Orientales" on 14 January 1829.

Victor Hugo, whom the Azerbaijani readers know as the author of novels, is also a great poet.

The poet, who started writing his poetry at the age of thirteen and thus earned the title of "the master of poetry", wrote "The Odes" (1822), "Autumn Leaves" (1831), "The Rays and Shadows" (1840), "The Inner Voices" (1837), "The Revenge" (1853), "The Audience" (1856), "The Horrible Year" (1871) and finally, in 1859-1870 the poetic works "The Legend of the Ages" in four volumes. For the sake of comparison, it should be stated that Hugo is the author of 20-volume novels, whereas his poetry books comprise 26 volumes.

Hugo's book "Les Orientales" was published in 1829. But what was the reason behind that appeal to the Oriental theme?

Many researchers, who bear the feeling of rancour against the Turks, consider the Turkish-Greek war (1821-1829) ongoing in that period to be the main reason for the creation of "Les Orientales". Or, when speaking about this work of the poet, they try to present it in such a way as if this book consisted of the poems dedicated to the Turkish-Greek war, that is, the poems targeted at the Turks.

LES
ORIENTALES,

PAR VICTOR HUGO

CINQUIÈME ÉDITION

TOME III

PARIS
CHARLES GOSSELIN, LIBRAIRE

HECTOR BOSSANGE,

Şairin "Şərq motivləri"
"Les orientales" du poète

Certainly, this "rancorous attitude" is not recent. This was the continuation of the attitude targeted at the Turks that existed for many centuries, during the crusade in 1096-1270, especially following the collapse of the Byzantine Empire and the formation of the Ottoman Empire.

Back in the XII century, the Pope of Rome would send orders in all directions and call for "the sacred war" against "infidel" Turks.

Many Medieval works describe the Turks only in battlefields. According to some Western sources, for a long time the Turks had been described as "wild" in Europe. However, the great personalities of Europe would express their scathing opinion against false attitudes. Voltaire's opinion is typical in this regard. "The Turks would not treat the Christians wildly as we always think of it and imagine it. The Turks would allow all the Greeks to build churches most of which were collegial".

The Turks would treat violently neither the population nor the historical monuments in the areas they occupied.

Even after the invasion of Constantinople, Sultan Mohammad II declared himself the protector of the Greek Church.

Owing to the Turks' sincere attitude, the Greeks preferred them to the Pope of Rome.

The statue erected to Sultan Salim in Hungary proves that with their raids the Turks have brought also culture to Europe.

It should be mentioned that Hugo's works could not have passed over the Turkish-Greek war either. Since, this war was in the focus of attention of all the European countries. Especially, Byron's death in the city of Missolonghi (of Greece) on 19 April 1824 started as if a new stage of the war and further inflamed the sparkle against the Turks in the Western countries.

As Hugo pointed out, the entire Europe encountered Byron's death as a common sorrow, general misfortune and national mourning.

In this sense, Hugo's writing poems related to the Turkish-Greek war was not a coincidence. The French writers Delfine Gueux, Alphonse de Lamartine, Casimir Delavigne also wrote poems related to the Greek struggle.

However, the idea that the Turkish-Greek war was the main reason for the creation of Hugo's "Les Orientales" is nothing but an idea completely false and biased. Since, prior to the outbreak of the war, back in the XIX century a great many works were created on the theme of the East (Byron, Goethe).

What was behind the creation of these series?

To this question, Hugo himself had the best answer: "This period sees the unprecedented involvement in the East. The study of the East has never developed so much before. They are now specialists in the Oriental Studies, whereas under Louis XIV (1643-1715 – A.Z.) they were Hellenists".

When speaking about Goethe's "West-Eastern Diwan", the eminent scholar Braginski wrote expressing his opinion about the reasons for the XIX-century European poets' appeal to these themes, "The Eastern exotics "Orientalism", as it is known, was one of the literary devices of the Romantics".

In the outstanding French writer Andre Maurois' words, "The East was in fashion in this period".

What sources did Hugo suggest while creating "Les Orientales"?

A.Maurois points out that there were enough sources to create the Oriental theme: the Bible, the scholar in Oriental studies Ernest Fuine, Byron's poems, above all, Spain, whose Romainseraux the poet recalls singing.

Some researchers suggest that Hugo learnt from Byron and Goethe. However, besides all this, he was aware of the Oriental sources used by Voltaire as well as Al-Kuran, the works by Sadi, Hafiz, Jalaladdin Rumi, Firdowsi. By the way, it should be noted that Sadi's work "Gulustan" was translated into French in 1634, and Andre du Ryer translated Al-Kuran into French in 1647.

Firdowsi's work "Shahnameh" translated into English by W.Johnson in the XVIII century was long afterwards also translated into French (1830-1878) by J.Malya and published in five volumes in Paris.

In his article about Byron, Hugo's reference to the Oriental byword was due to such awareness, "When the drop falls into the sea, it turns into a pearl".

Even some traces prove his awareness of the Eastern mythology and its separate Turkish branch.

Byron's "Oriental Tales" consists of six works: "The Giaour", "The Bride of Abydos", "Corsair", "Lara", "The Siege of Corinth",

"Parisina". Goethe divided his "West-Eastern Diwan" into twelve main parts: "The Tale of the Singer", "The Tale of the Wine-bearer", etc. Whereas Hugo had none of these divisions. The researchers divide the poet's "Les Orientales" into three relative parts: Turkish-Greek, Arabic-Persian and Spain.

Willing or unwilling, the reader is sure to think over a question: Why Spain? The poet himself answers the question, "Since, Spain is also the East: Spain is half African and Africa is half Asian". As it is known, the Oriental culture has mainly spread to Europe through Spain.

After the Moors invaded Spain in 711-714, they considerably developed culture there. They ruled this area approximately seven hundred years. This government even began to be known as the Arabic Spain. Of two major scientific centres of the Medieval Arabic culture, one was Baghdad and another, Cordova, the capital of Spain. While Europe was embraced by wild ignorance and strife all over, it was this kingdom (Cordova – A.Z.) alone that held the bright torch of ethics and culture before the Western world.

Thus, the profound representation of the Oriental culture in the ancient cities of Spain was not a coincidence. As Hugo stated, "The Mosque in the Gothic style erected in the ancient, beautiful city and the Eastern mosque with tin and bronze minarets among the fig and pine trees at the other edge of the city... The Kur'anic verses inscribed on all the doors, the sanctuaries where the floors and walls were dazzling with mosaics".

A.Maurois noted that these features were stronger in Grenade than Istanbul.

Thus, through all this, Hugo indicated the high status the Eastern culture enjoyed in Spain.

Hugo's "Les Orientales" includes poems that are on typical Oriental themes. His poem "The Djinns" is one of them.

The concept of "a djinn" as an output of the Oriental mythology, that is, Arabic mythology was later disseminated also among the other nations who adopted Islam.

This character deeply rooted in the monuments of folklore ("The Arabian Nights") gradually entered the written French literature as well.

Hugo introduced it to French poetry. The djinns are usually described to be invisible, only their actions are perceived. Hugo also describes them in this very way.

'Tis the Djinns' wild streaming swarm
Whistling in their tempest flight;
Snap the tall yews 'neath the storm,
Like a pine flame crackling bright.
Swift though heavy, lo! their crowd
Through the heavens rushing loud
Like a livid thunder-cloud
With its bolt of fiery might!

"The muse of poetry" Alphonse de Lamartine wrote to Hugo in his letter in April 1828 expressing his opinion about the poem "The Djinns", "This is the game of mind, however, generally taken, you didn't need it".

In his poem "Zara the Bather", the poet reveals the features in a beautiful girl's nature,

In a swinging hammock lying,
Lightly flying,
Zara, lovely indolent,
O'er a fountain's crystal wave
There to lave
Her young beauty-see her bent.
What doesn't go through the mind of
      this taintless beauty?
"Oh, were I a capitana,
Or sultana,
Amber should be always mixt
In my bath of jewelled stone,
Near my throne,
Griffins twain of gold betwixt.

"Then my hammock should be silk,
White as milk;
And, more soft than down of dove,
Velvet cushions where I sit
Should emit
Perfumes that inspire love.

Two kinds of beauty are not always found together. Zara is, at the same time, extremely lazy. Laziness and friskiness are characteristics of most of the beauties. However, it is interesting that Zara admits her own laziness.

A wise man said, "When a stupid says, 'I am a stupid man', he decreases his stupidity a bit; however, even if a lazy man admits his laziness, he still remains to be lazy".

The poet described the industrious people who love labour. They are Zara's friends.

Lazy and industrious people, the two contradicting, opposite poles like day and night, one of the colourful features of life.

Zara wanted to be a Sultan's wife, and what does the Sultana, the Sultan's wife think?

The Sultana (in the poem "The Moonlight") is not a frivolous lady who spends her life in golden waters. She is a romantic woman who can enjoy life.

She is absorbed in her realm of dreams watching the sea stretching along the shore, the moonlight dancing in the waters, dozing islands, the white patterns touching the rocks.

Captivity: Women's captivity. How can the burden of this captivity be measured? Certainly, in their minds the captives have many dreams which might be realized or not. However, one dream never leaves them: Motherland. And she wanted to realize the dreams of her mind. However... If she were not a captive.

One of the interesting points in "Les Orientales" is the poet's choice of epigraphs appropriate to the content of each poem. For instance, in the poem "The Djinns" Hugo picked out the words from Dante's comedy "The Divine", "As soon as the cranes set their long train in the air, they will sing their soothing songs full of moaning, so I noticed this moaning stretching in the attractive shadows parting from this storm".

The citation from the comedy "The Divine" as an epigraph to the poem is not a coincidence.

Since, these works are close to each other by nature. Or the words "The birds' song as harmonious as poetry was heard" quoted from Sadi's "Gulustan" in the work "The Captive" accomplish the captive's touchy song.

The poet's verse "The Veil" is one of the poems demonstrating the Oriental character, the features peculiar to the East to their subtleties. Hugo took Shakespeare's line "Have you prayed to-night, Desdemona?" as an epigraph to this poem. The entire essence, strength, enormousness of the great English writer's immortal work "Othello" was as if built on this line. "Have you prayed to-night, Desdemona?" This is the point when Othello, whose eyes are as furious as those of a tiger out of jealousy, distrust, and thus see nothing for fury, would strangle Desdemona in her bed a little later.

The epigraph, which Hugo cited from Shakespeare, informs the reader in advance, though not exactly, about the content or the end of the poet's verse "The Veil".

"...The girl enters. She sees her brothers in a furious state and asks in panics,

> What has happened, my brothers? Your spirit to-day
> Some secret sorrow damps
> There's a cloud on your brow. What has happened? Oh, say,
> For your eyeballs glare out with a sinister ray
> Like the light of funeral lamps.
> And the blades of your poniards are half unsheathed
> In your belt—and ye frown on me!
> There's a woe untold, there's a pang unbreathed
> In your bosom, my brothers three!

Eldest brother

> Gulnara, make answer! Hast thou, since the dawn,
> To the eye of a stranger thy veil withdrawn?

Thus, the trace of the events begins unfolding, now the reason for fury gradually clears out.

His sister states that she has gone to the bathhouse today, hidden from the sharp looks of the Moors and Albans and that she was covered with her veil while passing by the mosque. However, she says, she unfolded for a moment her veil as the afternoon heat was stifling her,

The sister

As I came, oh, my brother! at noon—from the bath—
As I came—it was noon, my lords—
And your sister had then, as she constantly hath,
Drawn her veil close around her, aware that the path
Is beset by these foreign hordes.
But the weight of the noonday's sultry hour
Near the mosque was so oppressive
That—forgetting a moment the eye of the Giaour—
I yielded to th' heat excessive.

Second brother

Gulnara, make answer! Whom, then, hast thou seen,
In a turban of white and a caftan of green?

The sister starts to stutter:

The sister

Nay, *he* might have been there; but I muflled me so,
He could scarcely have seen my figure.—
But why to your sister thus dark do you grow?
What words to yourselves do you mutter thus low,
Of "blood" and "an intriguer"?
Oh! ye cannot of murder bring down the red guilt
On your souls, my brothers, surely!
Though I fear—from the hands that are chafing the hilt,
And the hints you give obscurely.

Third brother

Gulnara, this evening when sank the red sun,
Didst thou mark how like blood in descending it shone?

The verdict of death has already been given. At this point, the ideas straddle, "Have you prayed to-night, Desdemona?" Now the final decision is clear.

The sister realizes that she is living her last and that it is time to say good-bye to life. Nevertheless, she begs her brothers; her begging resembles the last straw,

The sister

Mercy! Allah! have pity! oh, spare!
See! I cling to your knees repenting!
Kind brothers, forgive me! for mercy, forbear!
Be appeased at the cry of a sister's despair,
For our mother's sake relenting.
O God! must I die? They are deaf to my cries!
Their sister's life-blood shedding;
They have stabbed me each one – I faint – o'er my eyes
A *veil of Death* is spreading!

The brothers

Gulnara, farewell! take *that* veil; 'tis the gift
Of thy brothers – a veil thou wilt never lift!

In both "Othello" and the poem "The Veil" the incident of murder takes place approximately at the same time – after the evening. "The night is pregnant, who knows what it will bear tomorrow?"

Jealousy is a feature settled in the blood of the East, which is due to the strength of love. The Oriental man is so sensitive that he can immediately notice "the trace of an alien look on the face of his beloved".

It reminds us a *bayati* [a piece of Azerbaijani folk poetry],

Язизим бахды йарым

Юмрцмцн тахты йарым

Цзцндя эюз изи вар,

Сяня ким бахды йарым.

> Oh my dear, my luck
> You are the throne of my life
> There is a trace on your face,
> Who has looked at you?

However, unlike "Othello", in the verse "The Veil" the incident appears more clearly. The sister admits taking off her veil. Certainly, this would cause rumours and harm the brother's honour.

Their sister is not Hugo's Fantine. Fantine, who yielded to the adventurous mystery of youth, finds out that she is pregnant".

In the Western realm, there lives a Fantine, who gives birth to a child out of wedlock and makes efforts to grow it up.

However, in this environment – in the environment of the veil there is no room for Fantines.

And the brothers consider the murder of their sister as the only solution. It should be reminded that Othello, who strangled Desdemona, was also the son of this environment. That is why, he couldn't have chosen some other way. There is an attitude to a woman's wearing a veil and walking with her face covered in Byron's "Oriental Tales" as well,

> (Woe to the head whose eye beheld
> My child Zuleika's face unveil'd!)

Or

> To meet the gaze of stranger's eyes
> Our law, our creed, our God denies;
> Nor shall one wandering thought of mine
> At such, our Prophet's will, repine:
> No! happier made by that decree,
> He left me all in leaving thee.

The answer to the question is partially revealed In the first two lines: "The girl's appearance before the stranger will taint the parent's honour". The following line states the law of the Shariah. "It is a sin to appear before a stranger". What if she appears? The answer to this question raised in Byron's "The Bride of Abydos" is revealed in Hugo's "The Veil". Appearing before the stranger's eyes, taking off the veil results in the girl's death.

The works belonging to the East should be analyzed through the Oriental vision. For instance, some researchers (B.N.Kolesnikov) analyze Byron's poem "Gavour" as follows, "It turns out Gavour passionately loves Leila, and Leila is devoted to him. Gavour was all embraced in delight and happiness. However, Leila's jealous and cunning husband Hassan spies his wife and kills her treacherously".

How could it be otherwise?

By killing his treacherous, unfaithful, cunning, unprincipled, treasonous wife, Hassan lives. More precisely, he earns the right to live with dignity in life. The East can love and also kill and destroy if need be.

Along with being jealous, the Oriental man is both passionate and lustful. He is ready to sacrifice everything for this passion and lust.

Hugo's poem "Sultan Ahmad" is typical from this point of view. He cites Hafiz' words "Oh angel girl, let me tie your arms round my neck" as an epigraph.

The Turkish man Sultan Ahmad falls in love with the merry beauty of Grenade, who can sing well.

He offers the Spanish beauty his readiness to sacrifice Madina, where his power was most concentrated, for his love. And what place? Madina, which is one of the most sacred places in the Muslim realm.

One can perceive Hafiz' creative impact on Hugo's poem "Sultan Ahmad". Especially, this poem reminds us of Hafiz' ghazal [an Oriental form of poetry] beginning with the couplet "If that Turkish beauty yielded to us, I would cast away the cities of Samargand and Bukhara for her dark mole" narrating Teymour the Lame's offer.

The "Christian" beauties, who are well aware of the Oriental men's passion, try to realize all their wishes making use of these men's "weak point", and most of the time succeed in it. And the beauty of Grenade is also one of them. In answer to Sultan Ahmad's offer, she says,

"Be a Christian, noble king!
For it were a grievous thing:
Love to seek and find too well
In the arms of infidel.
Spain with cry of shame would ring,
If from honor faithful fell."

Sultan Ahmad is ready to fulfill Jouane's any order on condition that she gives her consent. At this point Jouane resembles Khumar, and Sultan Ahmad, Sheikh Sanan. The cross leads Sheikh Sanan to shepherding.

However, Sultan Ahmad does not descend to Sheikh Sanan's level, is not belittled to that extend. He confines himself to telling Jouane, "If you want, I can use your necklace like hand-beads".

"By these pearls whose spotless chain,
Oh, my gentle sovereign,
Clasps thy neck of ivory,
Aught thou askest I will be,
If that necklace pure of stain
Thou wilt give for rosary."

Sultan Ahmad is not belittled like Sheikh Sanan. Most probably, his title as Sultan, his background do not allow this.

The poem "Lovely Sultana" resembles the poem "Sultan Ahmad" in content. While the former is in the form of a dialogue, in "Lovely Sultana" all the ideas are stated by the Sultan.

Sultan has fallen in love with a Jewish beauty and wants to make her a sultana or worth for the Shah.

What doesn't the Sultan promise the Jewish beauty just to join her? – the world, his life, crown and people who trembles in his presence.

It becomes clear from the work that the Sultan is ruling a major part of the East. He is ready to give to the Jewish beauty Istanbul, Bursa, Mousoul, Trabson, Gang if only she gave her consent.

Since, "the Sultan needs the Sultana like a sword needs a pearl".

The poet's verse "Lazara" is also of this range. The researcher E.Evnina, who speaks of this poem, writes that the appearance of the old pasha willing to give numerous jewelry items, his wealth to a young girl is very surprising.

This case is neither surprising nor shocking for the Eastern realm. Irrespective of their age, like Hafiz, it is natural and typical for an

Easterner to give all his wealth to beautiful girls. However, the poet describes the beauty's contours more vividly in this poem.

The Turkish-Greek war constitutes one more branch of Hugo's Oriental verses. The poet wrote in the Introduction of his book in this connection, "A little earlier, for the West, like for its literature, the East could possibly have played a part of an example for empires too".

The Greeks' unforgettable war targeted all the nations at this direction, already.

In this period, France itself was in a hard situation. The riot against the dynasty of the Bourbons (1814-1830) embraced the entire country, and this dynasty was enjoying the last years of its reign. Soon the ministers were to sit before the court. However, leaving aside the struggles, chaos, strife within France, Hugo was writing poems about the Turkish-Greek war, to be more precise, against the Turks.

Hugo is a great artist and had a huge creativity. He is one of the unique figures of world literature. Nevertheless, he was the son of Europe. Europe's crusade targeted at the Turks had an impact on the young poet too.

Certainly, invasion is invasion. We do not intend to justify the invasion. However, as noted by Voltaire, the Turks let the Christians to practice their customs and traditions in the countries they "invaded".

Most probably, the Western countries acted so much assiduously, because they were against invasion as a whole. How many colonies did European countries take in this period? There is no need to list them.

It is enough to mention just one. Why didn't they speak about India that was moaning in the hands of England? Why did they keep mum?

Everything is clear.

In his poem "Enthusiasm" Hugo calls his friends to free Greece, this land and its martyr people saying, "To Greece, to Greece".

When should we set off? The poet answers his own question, "Tonight, tomorrow is too late".

He calls the emigrant Fave to give them commands. He says, "Let the battle music wakening the French bayonets long asleep sound, let the swords, bullets and shells work, let the horses be saddled".

The poet wants to be in the first rows of the battle and see all the events with his own eyes.

What does Hugo want? He wants to see the air clear, the meadows, mountains, forests quiet, and the beaches merry. It is a nice dream. If only this dream were not limited to Greece only and embraced all the colonial countries. If only it were not limited to religious fanaticism.

The poem "The Infant" holds a special place among the works Hugo wrote on this theme. The epigraph "Oh, horror, horror" he cites from Shakespeare's work "Macbeth" foretells about the horror to be described in the poem.

– The Turks have passed through those places. Those places are in ruins and mourning now. That is the wine island Chios. This island, which amazes with its natural beauty, is empty. No, it seems not completely empty. A blue-eyed Greek child is sitting at the bottom of the wall with his head leaned down. He is ready to defend his Motherland with a weapon in his hand,

> "Soft and sweet urchin, still red with the lash
> Of rein and of scabbard of wild Kuzzilbash,
> What lack you for changing your sob –
> If not unto laughter beseeming a child –
> To utterance milder, though they have defiled
> The graves which they shrank not to rob?
> "Would'st thou a trinket, a flower, or scarf,
> Would'st thou have silver? I'm ready with half
> These sequins a-shine in the sun!
> Still more have I money – if you'll but speak!"
> He spoke: and furious the cry of the Greek,
> "Oh, give me your dagger and gun!"

It should be reminded that the lesson "the Turks taught to this island, which supported Greece had a strong resonance in Europe, even the famous French artist, Hugo's friend E.Delacroix created the portrait "The Massacre of Chios" in 1823-1824. The poet could not stay indifferent to the theme that had turned into an important event.

The verse "Darwish" is one of Hugo's poems dealing with the Turkish-Greek war. The work speaks of a darwish's open protest against the tyranny of Ali Tepeleni (1741-1822), the ruler of the Yanina kingdom, who was both capable and cruel.

It should be stated that this ruler established his power in the city of Tepelen, occupied a great part of Greece later. Back in his lifetime there were many stories of the cruelty of Ali Pasha, who once hosted Byron. No doubt, it was rather exaggerated. It seems the entire Europe was aware of his cruelty. Hugo's writing a poem on this theme proves this idea. The poet depicts this tyranny, this cruelty through an old darwish.

Once Ali was walking along the road; the proud heads bowed to him bending till their feet. The entire crowd said, "Allah". Suddenly a darwish addressed him coming out of the crowd and holding the horse by the bridle.

Ali Tepelini, light of all light,

Who hold'st the Divan's upper seat by right,

Then he starts to interpret the main idea with sharp, insulting words,

An unseen tomb-torch flickers on thy path,

Whilst, as from vial full, thy spare-naught wrath

Splashes this trembling race:

These are thy grass as thou their trenchant scythes

Cleaving their neck as 'twere a willow withe—

Their blood none can efface.

But ends thy tether! for Janina makes

A grave for thee where every turret quakes,

And thou shalt drop below

To where the spirits, to a tree enchained,

Will clutch thee, there to be 'mid them retained

For all to-come in woe!

"Then you, Ali Pasha, will change your name like a dirty Jew while dying to deceive the black angel in the afterlife". Even to show the severity of his crime he says, "Allah keeps an iron yoke under the tree in the seventh layer of Jehenna loaded with godless souls". Ali Pasha listened to the old man till the end and gave his gown to him taking it off".

Several points should be taken into account here.

First, the poem proves that Hugo was well aware of the Muslim world, Islam.

Second, the poet shows that Ali Pasha has not lost his humanism, no matter how cruel he is. He could have killed the darwish with his weapon, his sword. On the contrary, for telling the truth he a kind of rewards him. There is a delicate essence felt here. He may have understood now that the crimes in the country are committed by those around him.

An affinity is felt between this poem and the story "The Epic of the Cruel Padishah and Zahid" from Nizami's "The Treasure of Mysteries". In both the works, under the threat of their death the old darwish and Zahid tell the truth to the ruler as it is, that is, reveal their cruelty.

Hugo devoted a poem to Missolonghi notorious for Byron's death in connection with the Turkish-Greek war. The poet calls all to defend this city "Missolonghi, let us drive them away, their strong ships, anchored fleet". The poet deals with the Turkish-Greek war in the verses "The Turkish March", "The Heads of Harem", "Naverain". These series of Hugo's poems have only one goal: to free Greece.

A branch of Hugo's "Les Orientales" is related to Spain. The poet writes that the East starts from China and stretches to Egypt. However, he did not confine himself to those geographic boundaries and included a country once known as Arabic Spain into his Oriental collection. Spain, which represented the Arabic culture wonderfully, was the only country among the places described in "Les Orientales" where the poet had been. In connection with Hugo's father General Sigisbert's military service in 1811, they lived there for a year.

The poet's "Grenade", "Nourmahal the Red", "Moorish Romance", "The Shadow" and other verses are related to the life in Spain.

In the poem "Grenade" the poet praises the beauties of the Spanish city Grenade, where the Eastern culture had rooted, and reminds the Alhamra Palace (Red Tower) – a historical, cultural keepsake of the Moors to the country.

Grenade is that place where, at the time when the power of the Arab caliphate in the East and of the Moors in the northern part of Spain ended, the emirate survived two hundred years more and developed their cultures. In Spain the long-term presence of the Moors with strong culture in power had naturally a strong impact on the indigenous people of the country as well. The Spanish romances appeared under the impact of the Moorish romances, and it is not a coincidence that for centuries (even after the Moors had been ousted from Spain) the romances belonging to the two nations coexisted and were spread being used in parallel. The Spanish romances were first translated into French by the poet's brother Abel Hugo in 1921. Hugo must have been under the impact of these romances when creating his "Moorish Romance". The poet wrote his poem "The Lost Battle" under the impact of "The General Romainseraux" (the Spanish and Moorish romances) too.

The romance describes Rodrigue's army helpless before the enemy.

He leaves the camp unaccompanied, all alone and ascends a very high hill, watches the place where his army was devastated, a river is flowing through that place covered in blood. He cries and says, "Yesterday I was the king of Spain, today I don't have a single city. Yesterday I had cities, today I have nothing. Yesterday I had palaces, servicemen, today I am alone".

Hugo conveys almost the same idea through the Turk Rashid.

But yesterday, and I had towns, and castles strong and high,
And Greeks in thousands, for the base and merciless to buy.
But yesterday, and arsenals and harems were my own;
While now, defeated and proscribed, deserted and alone,
I flee away, a fugitive, and of my former power,
Allah! I have not now at least one battlemented tower.

In the evening of his defeat, Rashid supposedly narrated like that and recalling his quite recent past, cried feeling the bitterness. Certainly, it was a poet's imagination rather than the truth. Since, first of all, the Turkish-Greek war had not finished yet; secondly, long after this, the Ottoman Empire would keep its "hand shade" on a number of Asian and European countries.

Opinions about Hugo's "Les Orientales" appeared prior to its publication as a book which admired his contemporaries: "Victor read to us unheard, completely unheard "Les Orientales"... There is not a single weak verse there" (Victor Pavi). However, the writer Andre Maurois distinguished those poems according to his views and outlook, though as a hypothesis. He noted, "the best of these verses ("Les Orientales" – A.Z.) is Hugo's poem "Ecstasy" isolated from the East, West, time, as well as space. The poet cites the words "And I heard a great voice" from "The Apocalypse".

I was alone beside the sea, one starry night.
With not a single wave or sail in sight.
Past the world's limits, stretched my eye,
And the forests and the mountains, with nature all 'round
Seemed united in questioning,in a vast yet mumbled sound,
the billows of the ocean, and the splendour of the sky.

The realm without troubles, sorrow. The moment and space the romantics love most: the starry night and the sea, also the shore bounding it. What must be the lonely man on the shore thinking? Where did his imagination take him? Which idea are "the eyes focused on the endless distance" tuned to?

In the Introduction to "Les Orientales" Hugo wrote, "The poet is free, let him choose his own way. No one has the right to restrict his imagination".

This idea was a kind of way the 27-year old young Hugo was showing to the future great Hugo. Neither his imagination, nor his creativity generated from this imagination was ever restricted by anything – poems, plays, novels, philosophical works. This unrestricted creativity led Hugo from French literary scene to the position in world literature.

As it is known, "Les Orientales" is related not only to the East.

Hugo's poem "Mazeppa" is also of this kind. However, this work has actually no relations to the East.

Hugo's "Les Orientales" enjoys a special place both among the works written on this theme in Europe and in the writer's own creative activities as a whole. It should be noted that back in the poet's lifetime this work was repeatedly published. "Les Orientales" was always highly appraised by the French literary scholars. In his academic speech, Leconte de Lille, who was elected to replace Hugo in his position in the French Academy after the poet's death, called "Les Orientales" an exceptional poetic invention for all the coming generations".

That volume was translated into many languages of the world. Back in 1876 Hugo wrote, "The Sultan of Turkey Sultan V (Abdulhamid) has "Les Orientales" translated in Turkish".

The poet did not confine himself to "Les Orientales", re-appealed the Oriental theme in different poems. The poet's verses "The Persian Ruler", "I Had Never Seen Firdowsi" are typical in this regard.

In the former poem, Hugo sends the Persian rulers to Tiflis in summer and to Isfahan in winter – to the gardens of roses, to their shades scattering fragrance. Certainly, all this was the outcome of the poet's romantic realm and illusion.

Alternatively, in the poem "I Had Never Seen Firdowsi" Hugo twice meets spiritually with the great Persian poet Firdowsi who lived eight centuries prior to him.

At the first meeting, the Persian artist was dressed in red. His head-gear was dazzling. At the second meeting, the poet was wearing a black vest. When asked about the reason, he answered, "You know I am fading away". Different moments of life – the heated moments and the moments of asceticism. And the poet's romantic vision of life.

We believe that Hugo's "Les Orientales" will be translated into Azerbaijani, and this theme will be re-appealed.

* * *

After "Les Orientales" Hugo turned to that theme again and wrote a number of works: "The Nine Years of Hijri", "Mohammad", "The Cedar", "The Gardens of Babylon", "The Egyptian Pyramids", "Zim-Zim", "1453", "Sultan Murad" and others. These works, no doubt, will turn into the target of research in future.

DID VICTOR HUGO ACCEPT ISLAM?

D ifferent ages have seen the French translation of a number of masterpieces of Oriental literature, and these translations have not gone without their influence on Western literature. On the other hand, most interestingly, some Oriental literary pieces, which first appeared in their French translations, have been translated into European languages via French rather than directly from their original versions. Among these works one can mention Saadi Shirazi's *Gulustan* (the translator is unknown) published in French in 1634, the famous Indian writer Pilpay's fables translated by David of Isfahan in 1644, *L'Alcoran de Mahomet* translated by Andre du Ryer in 1747, *The Arabian Nights Entertainments* translated by Antoine Galland (1704-1715), *Avesta* translated by Abraham-Hyacinthe Anquetil du Perron in 1771, *the Holy Qur'an* translated by Albin de Biberstein-Kazimirski in 1840. It is suffice to note that P.Posnikov translated *the Holy Qur'an* into Russian at the initiative of Peter I in 1716 having made use of its du Ryer's French translation. Also, K.Nikolayev's Russian translation of *the Holy Qur'an* from its Biberstein-Kazimirski's French translation was repeatedly published in Moscow (in 1864, 1865, 1876, 1880, and 1901).

According to the available facts, the most outstanding representative of the XVIII century French literature François-Marie d'Arouet Voltaire is so far considered the first writer who wrote about Prophet Muhammad's life and activities, *the Holy Qur'an* in French literature. That is, in his work *Essay on the Customs and the Spirit of the Nations* (1756) written on historical principles Voltaire widely dealt with Prophet Muhammad's life and *the Holy Qur'an* and expressed a high opinion about them.

This tradition was followed in the XIX century as well, and in his profound Preface to Biberstein-Kazimirski's translation and other works the outstanding French Oriental scholar Pyer Giyyom repeatedly returned to the theme related to the Prophet.

It is well known that the theme of the Prophet has repeatedly been referred to in the world literature as well as Azerbaijani literature. Among those authors one can mention Goethe, Pushkin, Lermontov, Husein Javid, Nabi Khazri, Zalimkhan Yagub.

Among the writers, who created works on this theme in French literature, one should specially underline the great French writer Victor Hugo who devoted three poetic pieces to Prophet Muhammad: 1. *Hijri NINE YEARS* 2. *Muhammad* and 3. *The Cedar*. The first work consists of 156 lines, the second 4 lines and the third 76 lines. These works have been studied by a young researcher Aygun Aliyeva from different aspects. According to the data obtained from some sources, more precisely, the French sources, the works *Hijri NINE YEARS*, *Muhammad* and *The Cedar*, which appeared in Hugo's book *The Legend of the Ages* published in 1859, had not been re-published until a century later following the French writer's centenary celebrated in 1902 – i.e. until 2002. There rises a natural question: Why? What was the reason for the concealment of these works from literary and scientific communities?

Some data we have lately obtained in French, the texts *Hugo Was a Muslim, Hugo – A Muslim? A Case of One Persistent Rumour, Abu Bakr Hugo*, the work *Hugo* by Mr. Han Ibrahim, the staff member of the former ENSUT University, ensuite l'Institut Supérieur de Gestion (ISG) facilitates the elucidation of the answer to this question.

Now again back to the question: "Was Hugo a Muslim?"

Some facts indicate that to solve this great problem, men from different scientific and professional spheres have been turned to, different forums and conferences have been held, and articles have been written. And naturally, each specialist has tried to substantiate his/her view. However, one issue is clear: "Although the French and Russian researchers and authors, who wrote about Hugo, repeatedly emphasized his Oriental poems that had allegedly been devoted to the Turkish-Greek war, none of them has said a word about his three works dedicated to Prophet Muhammad. Despite the regular reference to his book *The Legend of the Ages* published in 1859, those works, which first appeared in this collection, have completely remained out of focus. The researches and findings principally prove its being not a coincidence.

And now in reference to some sources related to Hugo's acceptance of Islam. It would be appropriate to state in advance that the views expressed in different texts available closely reiterate one another.

For instance, we think one can elucidate the idea by presenting the article *Hugo Was a Muslim* and the decision of Bladi forum which read: "The brightest of the poets, Hugo was a Muslim. No-one knew that the famous Hugo was a Muslim... No doubt, it was impossible to state in the media his being a Muslim..." Hugo, the author of these unparalleled poems, stated by admitting the path of faith that there is no

God but Allah alone, Allah has no companion and Muhammad is His messenger. Sheikh Ibrahim de TLEMCEN of Algeria, who was sent by Him (no doubt, it implies, by the Lord – A.Z.) on 6 September 1881, visited his apartment (Hugo's room – A.Z.) in Paris and consequently, the French author adopted the name of Abu Bakr Hugo. When visiting Hugo in Paris, Sheikh Ibrahim brought him a prayer rug. In 1885 he died as a Muslim. However, the frank-masons at the head of the III Republic arranged his funeral at the Pantheon of Paris. Thus, they managed to reach the only goal - to conceal his being a Muslim from the world".

The researches repeatedly emphasize that Hugo was an extreme, very determined Muslim and passed away as a Muslim.

The researches refer to Henri Guillemin's work *Hugo*, which state that the work starts with the following words that have the same tone today as well, "I do not know myself: I am closed to myself, only God knows who I am and how I am called".

How did Hugo turn to accept Islam?

Some researches indicate that after his daughter Leopoldine's drowning in the River Seine on 4 September 1843, Hugo started to familiarize himself with different religions and books related to them. One can assume that the French writer had profoundly known Islam since then.

However, we think Hugo familiarized himself with *the Holy Qur'an* after its translation by Biberstein-Kazimirski, made use of it in his works and later created some works under its impact. Most probably owning to his belief in the existence of the afterlife presented in Islam, he said in one of his poems dedicated to the death of his daughter and son-in-law,

Do rest, oh, my dear son, do rest, oh, my dear daughter
Be happy within the tomb!

A question may arise: "When did Hugo accept Islam?"

Evidently, the hitherto referred studies do not disclose the answer to this question. However, according to some writings, the answer to the question can approximately be identified.

The poem *Hijri NINE YEARS* ends as follows, "Victor Hugo, 15 January 1858" which implies that the work was accomplished on that date.

The researches explicate that long before Guillemin, on 23 May 1885 the newspaper *La Croix*, which was almost an official body of the French Catholic Party announced the day after the poet's death, "He has been insane for thirty years". We think this date "coincides with the time when *Hijri NINE YEARS* was written".

It seems Hugo had long accepted Islam by the time the Algerian Sheikh Ibrahim presented a prayer rug with Mecca's motif on it to the French poet during his visit to the poet's apartment in Paris.

The professor of the former ENSUT University, Mr. Han (Khan) Ibrahim's articles related to Hugo's acceptance of Islam also attract the attention with their austerity. Using a rhetorical question "Was Hugo a Muslim?", Han Ibrahim wrote that according to the will made up by Hugo on 31 August 1881, he had submitted all his manuscripts to Paris National Library – later on to be called the United European States Library.

Mr. Han Ibrahim wrote that all the unpublished works on Islam by this poet should be discovered, submitted to the UNESCO and that the ISESCO should make an initiative to protect these works so that the entire world can get acquainted with the works concealed in the true sense of the word for over hundred years.

According to the available facts, in 1902 Hugo's works on Islam were banned from appearance and concealed, and it was this period of time that Han Ibrahim implied when speaking of 'over hundred years'.

Further Han Ibrahim went on underlining that this famous, bright and radiant poet of Islam was born on Friday, 26 February 1802, fell ill on Friday 15 May 1885 and a week later, i.e. on 22 May, Friday, called Allah and passed away. Han Ibrahim pointed out separately that Friday is the greatest day of faith in Allah Who is alone and has no partners.

According to Han Ibrahim, when passing away, the poet's last words were the statement, "Allah has everything (Allah knows everything – A.Z.), there is nothing beyond Him, now I become His dear companion".

Expressing his opinion about Hugo's pseudonym, Han Ibrahim stated that the poet had adopted the name *Abu Bakr Hugo* with an intention of likening himself to the first caliph of Islam, whose name was Abu Bakr, and wrote in the late October 1883, "I know nothing more magnificent and higher than these words addressed by Abu Bakr to the believers (no doubt, he implied those who believed in Islam – A.Z.), "People, admirers of Muhammad, you should know that he has actually passed away. But whoever worships Allah should know that Allah lives, He never dies". Thus, return Abu Bakr Hugo to Muslims.

Mr. Han Ibrahim exENSUT, Gestion Superior Institute

It would also be appropriate to remind that views related to Friday and Hugo's pen-name is encountered in other sources as well.

Henri Guillemin wrote a book called *Hugo*, which caused a great sensation according to the available information. Some data provided there rouse a serious interest in a reader or researcher.

The repeated question "Was Hugo a Muslim?" is answered with new ideas. Especially for Azerbaijani readers and researchers.

It is noted on the basis of H.Guillemin's book that neither Hugo nor his two sons nor his grandchild was baptized or buried in a Christian style.

The statement of the software forum also notes that the author of these unparalleled poems (here the poems dedicated to Prophet Muhammad are implied – A.Z.) Hugo accepted that Allah is alone and without companions. Muhammad is His servant (messenger – A.Z.) and received the Algerian Sheikh Ibrahim de TLEMCEN, who was sent by Him, in his apartment in Paris on 6 September 1881 and assumed the pseudonym "Abu Bakr Hugo". In 1885 he died as a Muslim. However, the frank-masons at the head of the III Republic concealed his acceptance of Islam from the entire world by burying him at the Pantheon which was discovered only a century later. *La Croix*, the newspaper of the French Catholic Party wrote on 23 May 1885, i.e. the day after Hugo's death, "He has been insane for thirty years".

These evidences are repeatedly emphasized both in Bladi forum, the software forum, as well as in Henri Guillemin's monograph and Ibrahim Han's text. It should also be underlined that in Senegal Ibrahim Han published a series of articles on Hugo's acceptance of Islam.

In his book *Hugo* the French researcher Alain Decaux cited a quotation from the French writer, "I reject the church services, I appeal to all the souls. I believe in Allah". The last phrase is presented by the researchers as follows, "I believe in Allah – in a being Who is alone and without companions". The study also illuminates that Alan Decaux, the author of the work *Hugo* of over thousand pages is the ex-Minister responsible for Francophone.

The findings make us focus the attention to one more idea. The researches point out that the close people to Hugo would hear him to recite the following words from *the surah Fatiha* of *the Holy Qur'an* every day, "Indina – sira – tel – mustagim" (The Lord guides us on the right way). In the long span of time when he made this address his face would be covered in tears, and he would not bother the close people to him at all.

As Ibrahim Han wrote, Hugo had numerous poems on Islam, and published a series of poems on this theme, sometimes it is stressed that they exceeded one thousand. However, it is also underlined that the great majority of them were handwritten and did not appear in public, and were concealed for over a century. It is repeatedly stated that the world has been unaware of these poems by Hugo, and those manuscripts were given to the National Library of France, the future library of the United European States on 31 August 1881, and it is also persistently required that they should be disclosed.

According to the data obtained from the conducted researches, Arthur Rimbaud (1854-1891), Alphonse de Lamartine (1790-1869), Johann Wolfgang Goethe (1749-1832) also accepted Islam. The other texts related to Hugo's acceptance of Islam also add Napoleon Bonaparte's name (1769-1821) to the list. It is known that in 1819 Goethe wrote his famous *The West-östlicher Divan* and expressed high opinions about Prophet Muhammad in this work.

Lamartine had twice been to the East and wrote a number of poems on the Oriental theme. These poems reflected a high attitude to Prophet Muhammad as well. As mentioned earlier, Hugo also devoted poetic pieces to Prophet Muhammad. We think the positive values known to them from Islam made them turn to the theme. In both Lamartine's works and Hugo's poetry the statement "There is no god but Allah" is presented in a poetic form being accepted unequivocally.

As A.Aliyeva noted, Hugo reproduced some stories related to Prophet Muhammad's life in his poem *Hijri NINE YEARS* having studied his life to its nuances. The French writer found some resemblances between Prophet Muhammad's and his own lives. The researcher pointed out that Hugo sometimes presented some statements from *the Holy Qur'an* so poetically that it astonished the Tunisian scholar Afifa Marzuki.

A cedar. This word was brought to French poetry by Lamartine, and Hugo wrote a poem called *The Cedar*. As the Azerbaijani scholar indicated, it is clear from *the surah Al-Vagia* of *the Holy Qur'an* that the cedar is a tree growing in the Paradise. The cedar that found its reflection in Azerbaijani poetry eight centuries ago was brought to French poetry through Lamartine and Hugo's literary works, which substantially re-affirms that both the French writers were well aware of *the Holy Qur'an*.

It is most astonishing and contemplative that although both the French and Russian researchers speak of Hugo's some poems within his Oriental poetry dealing with the Turkish-Greek war by necessity or chance, neither Andre Besson, Andre Maurois, Pier Qamar nor the Russian researchers V.Paevskaya, N.Safronova, M.Treskunov and others mention a word about the French writer's poems dedicated to Prophet Muhammad, especially *Hijri NINE YEARS*, which is much more superior than those poems within the Oriental poetry referred above.

We think these thinkers found it advisable to admit Islam having seen Europe's riots, uprisings, revolutions, most probably unbearable life, intolerance disguised as religion.

Hugo's second poem *Muhammad* devoted to the Prophet consists of four lines. The Senegalese scholar Ibrahim Han wrote that it was impossible that Hugo, who admired Prophet Muhammad immensely, should devote to him only four lines all in all. The poem contains the following lines,

Muhammad who had a beautiful face would ride by turn
His mule Daidol and his donkey Yafur
By a mere chance he was wise
Both in his maturity and period of ignorance (childhood).

According to Ibrahim Han, this poem used to be very big, later disappeared or made lost by someone, and thus, only four lines remained.

One can also encounter the texts protesting the idea of Hugo's acceptance of Islam.

For instance, an article strikes the attention: *Victor Hugo – A Muslim? A Case of One Persistent Rumour*. The article starts with a rhetorical question: "Was Hugo a Muslim? Without hesitation some give a positive answer".

The text reads that Victor Hugo converted to Islam and asked to be buried in the big mosque in Paris. It is also noted here that when Hugo passed away, no mosque had been constructed in Paris yet. It is even compared with an imp hunting. Further it is stated that this rumour persistently wanders on the internet, anyone can google it by writing "Victor Hugo" Muslim.

The text presents also an extract from the internet site of the Amazagh bulletin, "A persistent rumour wanders among the Muslims that Victor Hugo admitted Islam. This rumour has appeared on the internet since the 11 September 2001 events. This is a variant of "Gusto rumour". They persistently confirm that he and some other famous people (Rimbaud, Lamartine, Goethe, Napoleon and others) were Muslims, however, the plot of their concealment (is ascribed to frank-masons) is aimed at damaging Islam. This text points out that in some Muslim circles this rumour was reiterated without being checked and tested, and being falsified and changed for over one century after

Hugo's death by the late XIX century the documents have been accepted by some of his interpreters, biographers and historians.

That idea was further continued to state that through rumours a real fact usually serves as a basis for a false outcome.

The presented views and refutations clarify the previous opinion. What does this statement "a real fact serves as a basis for a false outcome" imply? As a real fact it is stated irrefutably that in his book *The Legend of Ages* Victor Hugo created a series of poems some of which are the history of mankind. Among these poems there are pieces on *the Bible, the Gospel*, Jesus, Renaissance and some other poems... There are impressing poems on Islam and Muhammad here, including *Muhammad, Hijri NINE YEARS*. According to the author, on the basis of this simple fact the Muslims come to a conclusion that Hugo was not only a Muslim, but also drew away the jinn reciting the *surah Fatiha* and possessed a praying rug with Kaba's motif (picture – A.Z.) on it (performed prayers).

After all these views, we return to another problem specially striking in the article. Contrary to those who approve the "Hugo rumour" as the author calls it, here it is also reminded that Hugo, who died in 1885, had never asked to arrange his funeral services in the mosque in Paris. Designed thirty years earlier the Paris mosque was founded in 1820 (its opening ceremony took place in 1926). And as a conclusion, it is noted that the rumour spread widely and persisted. It will be further disseminated taken from the internet without any remarks. The pearl-divers will discover others through simple google searches.

In conclusion, it would be appropriate to express an opinion on an idea or two.

1.   The researcher writes that this issue began to appear on the internet following the 11 September 2001 events. As the studies indicate, in 1992 the study and cataloging of Hugo's works, especially the poems dedicated to Islam, mainly his manuscripts were banned, and only a hundred years later there appeared some chance to get familiarized with those works more or less.

2.   As it is noted, many monographs, scientific research works have been written on Hugo's literary works in French and Russian literary studies; unfortunately, no word has been said about these sophisticated works the great French writer dedicated to Prophet Muhammad. One of the astonishing features is that when speaking about the book *The Legend of the Ages*, those works, which appeared in that collection in 1857, are not mentioned at all.

3.   While Hugo's poetry was translated into Russian, those works escaped notice.

4.   All this confirms that, as the researchers note, Hugo's many works related to the Muslim realm are being kept in secret in the archives. As frequently emphasized, it is high time to discover them and start their researches.

5.   The fact of Hugo's acceptance of Islam in the works of some researchers seems more convincing than the arranged facts refuting it.

6.   While reading Hugo's works dedicated to Islam, one can witness how profoundly he knew *the Holy Qur'an* and the life of Prophet Muhammad. The French writer's works *Hijri NINE YEARS*, *The Cedar* are its apparent proof. It would be appropriate to mention that the title of the writer's second work was derived from the name of the cedar tree described in "the Paradise" reflected in the *surahs An Najm* ("The Star") and *Al Vagia* of *the Holy Qur'an*.

7.   When reading these works carefully, some details presented in them substantiate one's conclusion about Hugo's acceptance of Islam. They also repeatedly state that Abu Bakr Hugo is the very Victor Hugo.

8.   Some available facts confirm that 45 thousand people in the world accept Islam every year. Certainly, this is the information dating back to some 20-25 years, most probably now it is more than that. According to the findings from the researches, so far 177 thousand people in France have accepted Islam, which implies that the acceptance of Islam is not a new phenomenon for the world or France either.

9.   The issue of Hugo's acceptance of Islam is called "rumour". Those, who want to refute this issue, suspect also the acceptance of Islam by Rimbaud, Lamartine, Goethe, even Gusto. And what about the strongest boxer of the humanity Muhammad Ali, as well as Armstrong, Tyson, Ribery and many famous people whose names we fail to mention here. Are they "rumours" too?

10. We think Hugo's acceptance of Islam is not a problem, it is the reality. However, it is necessary and advisable to continue the researches further.

PhD. Asgar Zeynalov

THE OUTSTANDING FRENCH SCHOLARS AND INTELLIGENTSIA ON ASGAR ZEYNALOV

Jean Louis Bacque-Grammont
Director for the First-class Researches
At the National Centre for Scientific Research,
President of the International Committee
For Prior-and-During the Periods of the Ottoman Empire (France)

With great interest, I read Mr.Asgar Zeynalov's work "The East in French Literature" published in Azerbaijani-Turkish in Baku in 1996.

Despite the absence of necessary conditions and the lack of earlier researches, the author who has never been to France, nonetheless, speaks French, has managed to accomplish such a valuable work.

It would be more appropriate for the author to visit France in order to collect more important materials for his other new works and also increase his language experience.

We would like to focus the related French organizations' attention on the issue.

Baku, 26 September 1997

JEAN-LOUIS BACQUÉ-GRAMMONT
Directeur de Recherche de 1ᵉ Classe
au Centre National
de la Recherche Scientifique
Président du Comité International
d'Études Pré-Ottomanes et Ottomanes

16 avenue de la Gare
94370 SUCY-EN-BRIE
tél./fax : 01 49 82 59 67

J'ai consulté avec intérêt l'ouvrage
de M. Äskär Zeynalov, Fransız ädäbiy-
yatında Şärq (L'Orient dans la littérature française), publié en turc azéri à
Bakou en 1996.

Si l'on tient compte des conditions
peu favorables et du manque de docu-
mentation malgré lesquels ce travail
a pu être réalisé par un auteur francophone qui n'est jamais allé en France,
il y a tout lieu de croire qu'un séjour
dans ce pays lui permettrait non seulement de parfaire sa pratique linguistique, mais aussi de rassembler les
matériaux nécessaires pour la rédac-
tion d'autres ouvrages.

Nous attirons donc sur ce cas la
bienveillante attention des services
français concernés.

Bakou, le 26 septembre 1997

THE AZERBAIJANI RESEARCHER OF VICTOR HUGO'S WORKS AT THE LANGUAGE SKILLS CENTRE

PhD, Professor Asgar Zeynalov, Head of the Practical French Department (Azerbaijan University of Languages) has attended the in-service training at the *Centre* de Linguistique Appliquée (CLA) of the University of Franche Comte in the city of Bezanson, France. One of the most prestigious newspapers of France "L'Est Republicain" published an article about our compatriot.

The Azerbaijani Researcher of Victor Hugo's Creativity at the *Centre* de Linguistique Appliquée (CLA): Asgar Zeynalov, who teaches the XVII, XVIII and XIX-century French literature in Baku, is on a one-month visit to Bezanson. The mouth is not only for eating, but also for speaking. Yet, how to speak? This is the main issue. This is how Asgar Zeynalov, who is fond of frequently quoting aphorisms, thinks of Victor Hugo. This 55-year old, neatly-dressed gentleman teaches the XVII, XVIII and XIX-century French literature at Azerbaijan University of Languages in Baku, the capital of Azerbaijan.

The Happiest Man: This ancient country between the Caucasian Mountains and the Caspian has the population of eight million people. This country, which produces 1 million barrels of oil a day, has signed an unprecedented contract (with British Petroleum). Consequently, English is the first foreign language, and French is ranking second having ousted Russian. Although Asgar Zeynalov defended his dissertation on the theme "Voltaire's Oriental Creativity", the great Victor Hugo remains to be his favourite writer. He considered himself the happiest man during his visit on 4 August to the *Centre* de Linguistique Appliquée (CLA) in Bezanson together with his colleagues Elmina Asgarova amd Anar Hajiyev. Asgar Zeynalov had wished for 35 years to visit Victor Hugo's Motherland. Hence, with great pleasure he suggested to have photos taken at Victor Hugo's statue. The author of the books about Hugo has also translated his poetry, written Foreword to the Azerbaijani translation of "Les Miserables". Professor Zeynalov, who is an author of about 15 books, 250 articles, is the member of the Union of Writers and Journalists in his own country. His writings related to French literature have been published in Moscow and Iran too. He tells jokes related to Voltaire, who lived in the Ferney village mentioned in the works of Alexander Dumas, George Sand, Gustave Flaubert, Guy de Maupassant; nevertheless, he always returns to Victor Hugo. "I am well aware of the works of Byron, Goethe, and Shakespeare; nevertheless, for me there is only Victor Hugo in world literature". On 16 August Asgar Zeynalov will present a copy of his works before the registration of the city hotel to the authorities of the city executive power.

Daniel BORDUR
The newspaper "L'Est Republicain"
France, the city of Bezanson, 11 August 2007
(translated from French by the author).

Le spécialiste azéri de Victor Hugo au CLA

Pour un mois à Besançon, Asker Zeynalov enseigne la littérature française des XVIIe, XVIIIe et XIXe siècles à Bakou.

« La bouche ne sert pas seulement pour manger, mais aussi pour parler. Mais comment parler ? C'est le problème principal ». Ainsi devise Asker Zeynalov à propos de Victor Hugo dont il aime citer les aphorismes. Ce monsieur de 55 ans en costume strict enseigne la littérature française dès 17, 18 et 19e siècles à l'université de Bakou, la capitale de l'Azerbaïdjan, où vécut le grand joueur d'échecs Gary Kasparov.

« Le plus heureux des hommes »

Entre mer Caspienne et Caucase, cette ancienne république soviétique est peuplée de 8 millions d'habitants. Produisant un million de barils de pétrole par jour, le pays est traversé par un oléoduc géant et a signé un contrat mirifique avec BP. L'anglais y est désormais la première langue étrangère et le français a supplanté le russe... Asker Zeynalov a fait sa thèse sur les influences orientales de Voltaire, mais Victor Hugo est son écrivain préféré. Aussi, quand il a débarqué le 4 août dernier à Besançon, avec ses collègues Elmina Askarova et Anar Hadjiyev, pour suivre un stage au CLA, il s'est senti « le plus heureux des hommes ». Cela faisait 35 ans qu'il attendait ce voyage dans « la patrie de Victor Hugo ». Et c'est avec un plaisir visible qu'il annonce s'être fait photographier à côté de la statue de l'écrivain.

Auteur de livres sur Hugo, il a traduit ses poèmes, rédigé la préface de la version azéri des Misérables... Ayant publié une dizaine d'ouvrages et 250 articles, le professeur Zeynalov est membre de l'Union des écrivains et de l'Union des journalistes de son pays.

Il fait également autorité dans les cercles universitaires et francophiles de Moscou ou d'Iran. Outre l'auteur du Dernier jour d'un condamné, il a travaillé sur Alexandre Dumas, George Sand, Gustave Flaubert, Guy de Maupassant...

De Voltaire, il apprécie les fables tragiques. Non dénué de sens de l'humour, il lui a écrit à Ferney-Voltaire, près de Genève... Mais toujours il retourne à Hugo : « Je connais Byron, Goethe, Shakespeare, mais il n'y a qu'un Victor Hugo... »

Il attend avec une certaine fierté le 16 août et la réception des stagiaires du CLA à l'hôtel de ville pour remettre au maire un exemplaire de ses ouvrages.

Daniel BORDUR

Asker Zeynalov : « 35 ans que j'attendais ce voyage dans la patrie de Victor Hugo ».
Photo Patrick BRUMENT

« Je ne suis pas un homme politique »

Un entretien avec un intellectuel d'un pays n'ayant pas rompu avec l'autoritarisme politique est déroutante.

Il répond à des codes dont la clé est souvent difficile à trouver. Vos questions sortant des clous suscitent parfois un sourire désolé : « Je ne veux parler que de littérature », prévient Asker Zeynalov après qu nous l'ayons interrogé sur l'élection, en 2003, du président Ilham Aliev avec plus de 76 % des voix.

Il succédait alors à son père Gueida Aliev, ancien officier du KGB, moins en rités et les manifestations qui suivirent réprimées sans ménagement. Au parlement, les soutiens du président ont 114 des 125 sièges. En mars 2005, le journaliste critique Elmar Houseynov fut assassiné...

Que pense Asker Zeynalov du rôle politique que joua Victor Hugo en s'opposant à Napoléon III et le payant d'un long exil ? Réponse : « Il aurait fallu connaître Hugo de son vivant... On insiste sur la dissidence de l'écrivain. Réponse : « Je connais très bien la vie de d'amitié entre les peuples, on connaît davantage les grands écrivains que les noms des présidents »

Pardonnons à la langue de bois, elle peut aussi éviter quelques ennuis... Comme nous avons demandé aux stagiaires israéliens et palestiniens de quoi est fait leur quotidien, nous avons cherché à savoir comment on vit dans un pays où le cessez-le-feu de 1994 avec l'Arménie sur le Haut-Karabach n'a rien réglé ? Un pays dont les voisins russe et géorgien ne sont pas loin de s'invectiver ?

THE AZERBAIJANI SCHOLAR'S NEW SUCCESS

*L*ately the journal of the Society of Victor Hugo's Friends functioning in Paris has published an article about our compatriot PhD, Professor Asgar Zeynalov. The author of the article is the President of the Society, world-renowned Hugo scholar Arnaud Laster. It should be reminded that this is the second article about Professor Asgar Zeynalov published in France. The first article appeared on 11 August 2007 in the newspaper "L'Est Republicain".

Information Letter #481
The Society of Hugo's Friends
http//www.victorhugo.asso.fr
Secretariat: 7, place Salvador Allende, 94000 Creteil
amis.victor.hugo@gmail.com

The Azerbaijani University professor Asgar Zeynalov has communicated with us. He is the PhD on Voltaire's Creativity, member of the Azerbaijan Union of Writers and Journalists, author of a number of books and articles (about the works of La Fontaine, Voltaire, Hugo, Balzac, George Sand, Dumas, Maupassant and others), some of which have been published in Iran, Turkey and Moscow.

Most of his works are devoted to Hugo:
– The East in French Literature, 1996, 154 p.
– The reviewed edition in 1999, 164 p.
– The Translation from French into Azerbaijani of the Poetry of Victor Hugo and Louis Aragon, 2012, 81 p.
– Victor Hugo, 2001, 101 p. (in Azerbaijani and French)
– He Was a Century... 2010, 240 p.
– The Billionaire of French Literature (in French), Baku 2013, p.101.

As a specialist in world literature, he participated in the 6 August, 13 August and 3 September releases of the TV series "The Literary Monuments" (AzTV) dedicated to Victor Hugo's "Les Miserables". The first program was attended by a philosopher, who spoke of the philosophical aspect of the novel. The publication and translation of Hugo's novels and other works in Azerbaijan as well as the attitude to his works "Les Orientales" and "The Hunchback of Notre Dame" in France were also mentioned in the program. It also presented "Les Miserables" and "Claude Gueux" in comparison with his poetic works, the blessings of Jean Valjean to Cosette and of Hugo to his own daughter at their weddings as described in Hugo's poems dedicated to the memory of his daughter Leopoldine. Jean Valjean is analyzed together with the priest Myriel, Fantine, Javert, Cosette and Marius. There is also an attitude towards the nineteen-year conviction. The next project of the program is about Victor Hugo's poetry and "The Hunchback of Notre Dame".

Arnaud LASTER
President of the Society of Hugo's Friends
and the Festival of Victor Hugo and His Equals,
6 October 2013, Paris, France

THE OLD HUGO, UNIVERSAL WRITER

The author of many books and articles, scholar specialized in Hugo, Asgar Zeynalov has presented Hugo's "Les Miserables" published in Azerbaijani in both Latin and Cyrillic scripts to the museum. The University teacher from Baku, who visited the Centre for Language Use says, "I am the author of the monograph about Hugo. I have analyzed his poems on the Oriental theme, translated his verses from the original into our language and written articles on Balzac, Dumas and George Sand".

The newspaper "L'Est Republicain"
France, 24 July 2014

The Head of the Region of Franche Comte – Vice President Pierre Feysot's Letter to the Newspaper "L'Est Republicain"
Sender: magnin-feysot.pierre@orange.fr
Receiver:asgerzeynalov51@gmail.com
Mr. Zeynalov,
The copy of this message is sent to one of the correspondents of the newspaper "L'Est Republicain"
Original message
Hello, Marie Claire. I hope you are fine, Alfonse and you.
On 22 July in the regional council I received the French teachers visiting Language Skills Centre in Bezanson from all over the world, who teach French as a foreign language. Among them, Mr.Zeynalov from Azerbaijan has translated many novels of Hugo and written many books about the author, who was born in Bezanson.
Can the newspaper "L'Est Republicain" provide some space for a portrait essay on this person, an article related to his attitude to the French writer, French literature and the French language on its pages?

By sending this message to the authorized person from the editorial of Bezanson, presenting the interest of French literature, also the interest of the representative of Bezanson and Franche Comte, I express my opinion and deep gratitude.
Sincerely,

P.S. Mr.Zeynalov is leaving on Friday. Here are his contact details:
0695344939 asgerzeynalov51@gmail.com
29 July 2014

Professor Asgar Zeynalov's successive achievement is his book "Hugo – the Billionaire of French Literature" published in France. *Hugo – Milliardaire de la literature francaise", "Presses Academiques Francophone", France, 160. The related information prepared by the special correspondent of AzerTAC in France Asgar Aliyev has found its reflection in the newspapers "Respublica" and "Khalg". We are presenting the information here.*

http://azertag.az/xeber/845406
http://azertag.az/xeber/Fransada_azerbaycanli_edebiyyatsunas
_alimin_kitabi_nesr_olunub-845406 [A book by the Azerbaijani literary scholar has been published in France]

Paris, 10 April, AZERTAC The professor of Azerbaijan University
of Languages, known in scientific circles in France as a specialist in
Hugo, Ph.D. Asgar Zeynalov's book "Hugo – the Billionaire of French
Literature" describing the life and creative activity of the great French
writer, public figure Victor Hugo, whose works are read with great love
in Azerbaijan, has been released in the Publishing House "Presses
Academiques Francophone". The scientific editor of the 160-page book
published in French is Ph.D. Vazeh Asgarov and its reviewer is Professor Sevda Vahabova.

The book starts with the articles written at different times by the
world-known French scholars Jean Louis Bacque-Grammont and Arnaud Laster, along with the outstanding scholar in Western literature
Professor Jalil Naghiyev about Asgar Zeynalov, the author of the first
monographs about the French writers like Voltaire and Hugo in Azerbaijani literary studies. They highly appraised the scientific activity of
the Azerbaijani scholar specialized in Hugo.

The correspondent of the influential French newspaper "L'Est Republicain" Daniel Bordur's thoughts about the Azerbaijani scholar hold a
special place in the book, "Although Asgar Zeynalov defended his dissertation on Voltaire's Oriental works, the great Victor Hugo is his favourite writer. Owing to his translation, the Azerbaijani readers have
familiarized themselves with some samples of Hugo's poetry. He has introduced the Azerbaijani version of the writer's novel "Les Miserables".
Although he deals with the creative activities of Alexander Dumas,
George Sand, Gustave Flaubert, Guy de Maupassant, and Voltaire who
lived in the village of Ferney, he repeatedly returns to Victor Hugo, "I
am well informed about the creative activities of Byron, Goethe, and
Shakespeare; however, there is only one Hugo in world literature".

In the book, the author has dealt with the French writer's life and
creativity profoundly in the section "Hugo's Life". And the section
"Hugo and Azerbaijan: studies and translations" provides information
about Azerbaijani literary scholars and translators' appeal to Victor

Hugo's works at different times and the translation of his works into our mother tongue and their repeated publications. The book also focuses the attention on the facts that Hugo's novel "Les Miserables" and a little later his "Selected Works" were printed in Latin script. It is also stated that Asgar Zeynalov has written Forewords to both the books. A separate section is assigned to Hugo's poetry in the book to provide an analysis of the writer's "Oriental Verses" and his poems dedicated to the death of his daughter Leopoldine, who tragically drowned in the River Seine.

The section "Hugo's Novels" provides a profound analysis of the French writer's novels "Les Miserables" and "The Hunchback of Notre Dame" well known to Azerbaijani readers.

The section "Hugo's Contemporaries" constitutes the most interesting pages of the book. It presents the articles about the most outstanding representatives of the XIX-century French literature. These are basically the articles about Hugo's friends – Balzac, Dumas (Father), George Sand, Flaubert, and also Maupassant. The section "The Letters to and from Paris" consists of the correspondence between A.Zeynalov and Arnaud Laster, the French scholar specialized in Hugo. The section "Hugo's Friends" deals with the life, scientific and public activities of Arnaud Laster, President of the Society of Hugo's Friends.

A.Zeynalov's visits to France, his interesting meetings and unforgettable moments are described under the title "In Hugo's Motherland".

As it is obvious, the Azerbaijani scholar has proved himself as a specialist in Hugo not only in our Republic, but in France as well.

The publication of A.Zeynalov's work "Hugo – the Billionaire of French Literature" is a significant event in Azerbaijani literary studies.

It should be reminded that the monograph "Hugo - the Billionaire of French Literature" by Asgar Zeynalov, who is the author of over 25 books, over 350 scientific and journalistic articles, is his third book published abroad.

Asgar ALIYEV
Special Correspondent of
AZERTAC in Paris

BIBLIOGRAPHY

A.Zeynalov's Books on French Literature

1.   A.Zeynalov. "The East in French Literature", Baku, "Elm", 1996, 154 p. (in Azerbaijani)

2.   A.Zeynalov. "The East in French Literature", "Oghuz eli", 1999, 164 p. (reviewed edition, in Azerbaijani)

3.   A.Zeynalov. "The East in Voltaire's Works", The Publishing House of Azerbaijan National Encyclopedia, 2001, 160 p. (in Azerbaijani)

4.   A.Zeynalov. "Victor Hugo", Baku, "Mutarjim", 2001, 104 p. (in Azerbaijani and French)

5.   A.Zeynalov. "The Companion of Years", Baku, "The University of Economics", 2004, 245 p.

6.   A.Zeynalov. "Contemplations on Teaching Language and Literature", "Mutarjim", 2009, 116 p.

7.   Zeynalov A. "He Was a Century", Baku, "Mutarjim", 2010, 240 p. (in Azerbaijani and French).

8.   Zeynalov A. "The Translation of Victor Hugo and Louis Aragon's Verses from French into Azerbaijani", Translator – Asgar Zeynalov, Baku, "Mutarjim", 2012, 81 p.

9.   A.Zeynalov. "The Billionaire of French Literature", Baku, "Mutarjim", 2013, 101 p. (in French)

10.   A.Zeynalov. "Hugo", Baku, "Mutarjim", 2014, 412 p.

11.   A.Zeynalov. "Hugo", Baku, "Mutarjim", 2014, 468 p. (a reviewed edition) (in Azerbaijani and French)

12.   A.Zeynalov. "Hugo – the Billionaire of French Literature", France, "Presses Academiques Francophones", 2015, 160 p. (in French)

13.   A.Zeynalov. "1802 – the Century Was Two Years Old…". Baku, "Mutarjim", 2015, 204 p. (in French)

www.ingramcontent.com/pod-product-compliance
Lightning Source LLC
Chambersburg PA
CBHW050345290526
45785CB00006B/2646